THE CHILDREN'S SONGBOOK

Selected and arranged by
DONALD MITCHELL
and
RODERICK BISS

Illustrated by
ERROL LE CAIN

FABER MUSIC
in association with
FABER AND FABER
London · Boston

The Faber Book of Children's Songs
first published in 1970 by Faber & Faber Ltd
This new version, retitled,
first published in 1984 by Faber Music Ltd
in association with Faber & Faber Ltd
3 Queen Square, London WC1N 3AU
Printed in England by The Thetford Press Ltd
Thetford, Norfolk
All rights reserved

ISBN 0 571 10054 6

© *1970, 1984 by Donald Mitchell and Roderick Biss*

CONTENTS

PREFACE

The songs that we have so much enjoyed gathering together in this book are not all of them about children or childhood, and yet many of them have a childlike quality. It is in this sense that our title must be understood — songs which show the vividness, clarity and imagination we associate with childhood, and not least the qualities of charm and delight. If we look at our title in this light, then these are 'children's songs', but at the same time songs for all of us, children and adults, since we all retain — or hope to retain — the evocative experiences and perceptions of childhood in our adult life.

The songs that we have collected represent a means of handing down from generation to generation not only a rich harvest of incomparable tunes but also a wealth of human experience, because many of the songs are linked with historical incidents, national sentiment, work, play and human passions (both creative and destructive), the very stuff of life as it has been lived for centuries.

It has been our ambition to continue, and perhaps extend a little, the great tradition of children's song books. Old traditions tend to die if they are not continually re-interpreted and re-fashioned, and it is in the spirit of affectionate renewal that we have approached the songs in this book. We shall be well satisfied if our anthology reminds a fresh generation of the fund of musical invention that belongs to our communal musical memory.

Our arrangements should not be regarded as sacrosanct. Performers should feel free to adapt the settings to meet their own needs, writing, if they so wish, their own parts for instruments that may be available. Alternatively, the melodies may be sung unaccompanied. In short, we hope our book will stimulate performers to use their own imaginations in the widest possible way.

All the arrangements are by Roderick Biss but for the three settings of Australian songs, which have been arranged by Donald Mitchell.

T.R.B., D.M.

Yes, I ken John Peel, and Ruby too,
Ranter and Ringwood, Bellman and True,
From a find to a check, from a check to a view,
From a view to a death in the morning.
For the sound of his horn, etc.

Then here's to John Peel from my heart and soul,
Let's drink to his health, let's finish the bowl,
We'll follow John Peel thro' fair and thro' foul
If we want a good hunt in the morning.
For the sound of his horn, etc.

D'ye ken John Peel with his coat so gay?
He lived at Troutbeck once on a day,
Now he has gone far, far away,
We shall ne'er hear his voice in the morning.
For the sound of his horn, etc.

THE KEEPER

The first doe he shot at he missed;
The second doe he trimmed he kissed;
The third doe went where nobody wist
Among the leaves so green, O.
Jackie Boy!, etc.

The fourth doe she did cross the plain;
The keeper fetched her back again;
Where she is now she may remain
Among the leaves so green, O.
Jackie Boy!, etc.

The fifth doe she did cross the brook;
The keeper fetched her back with his crook;
Where she is now you must go and look
Among the leaves so green, O.
Jackie Boy!, etc.

The sixth doe she ran over the plain;
But he with his hounds did turn her again,
And it's there he did hunt in a merry, merry vein
Among the leaves so green, O.
Jackie Boy!, etc.

CHORUS

Jack-ie Boy! Mas-ter! Sing ye well? Ve-ry well! Hey down! Ho down!

Der-ry, der-ry down, A-mong the leaves so __ green, O. To my

hey-down, down. To my ho down, down. Hey down! Ho down!

Der-ry, der-ry down, A-mong the leaves so __ green, O.

★ If there are more than two voices available the 1st part should be sung by a group and the 2nd part by a solo voice.

9

'Oh, gay are the garlands and red are the roses
I culled from the garden to bind on my brow.
'*Oh, don't deceive me*,' etc.

Thus sang the maiden, her sorrow bewailing;
Thus sang the poor maid in the valley below.
'*Oh, don't deceive me*,' etc.

Green - sleeves was my heart of gold, And who but my La - dy Green - sleeves.

I have been ready at your hand,
To grant whatever you would crave;
I have both waged life and land,
Your love and good-will for to have.
Greensleeves was all my joy, etc.

If you intend thus to disdain,
It does the more enrapture me,
And even so, I still remain
A lover in captivity.
Greensleeves was all my joy, etc.

My men were clothed all in green,
And they did ever wait on thee;
All this was gallant to be seen;
And yet thou wouldst not love me.
Greensleeves was all my joy, etc.

Thou couldst desire no earthly thing,
But still thou hadst it readily,
Thy music still to play and sing;
And yet thou wouldst not love me.
Greensleeves was all my joy, etc.

Well, I will pray to God on high,
That thou my constancy mayst see,
And that yet once before I die,
Thou wilt vouchsafe to love me.
Greensleeves was all my joy, etc.

THE WEE COOPER OF FIFE

1. There was a wee coo-per wha lived in Fife, *Nick - e - ty, nack - e - ty, noo, noo, noo;* And he had mar-ried a gen - tle wife, *Hey, wil - ly, wal-lack - y, ho John Dou-gle A - lane, quo rush - i - ty roo, roo, roo.*

14

She would na bake nor would she brew,
Nickety, nackety, noo, noo, noo;
For spilin' o' her comely hue.
Hey, willy, wallacky, ho John Dougle
Alane, quo rushity roo, roo, roo.

She would na caird nor would she spin,
Nickety, nackety, noo, noo, noo;
For shamin' o' her gentle kin.
Hey, willy, wallacky, ho John Dougle
Alane, quo rushity roo, roo, roo.

The cooper has gone to his woo' pack,
Nickety, nackety, noo, noo, noo;
And he's laid a sheep's skin on his wife's back.
Hey, willy, wallacky, ho John Dougle
Alane, quo rushity roo, roo, roo.

'I'll no be shamin' your gentle kin,
Nickety, nackety, noo, noo, noo;
But I will skelp my ain sheepskin.'
Hey, willy, wallacky, ho John Dougle
Alane, quo rushity roo, roo, roo.

'O I will wash and I will spin,
Nickety, nackety, noo, noo, noo;
And think nae mair o' my gentle kin.'
Hey, willy, wallacky, ho John Dougle
Alane, quo rushity roo, roo, roo.

'O I will bake and I will brew,
Nickety, nackety, noo, noo, noo;
And think nae mair o' my comely hue.'
Hey, willy, wallacky, ho John Dougle
Alane, quo rushity roo, roo, roo.

A'ye what hae gotten a gentle wife,
Nickety, nackety, noo, noo, noo;
Send ye for the wee cooper o' Fife.
Hey, willy, wallacky, ho John Dougle
Alane, quo rushity roo, roo, roo.

The apples were ripe and ready to fall,
Hee-haw ready to fall,
There came an old woman to gather them all,
Hee-haw gather them all.

Oliver rose and gave her a drop,
Hee-haw gave her a drop,
Which made the old woman go hippety hop,
Hee-haw hippety hop.

The saddle and bridle they lie on the shelf,
Hee-haw lie on the shelf,
If you want any more you can sing it yourself,
Hee-haw sing it yourself.

- rov - ing with you fair maid.
- rov - ing with you fair A - maid.

The past six months I'd been to sea,
Bless you, young women;
The past six months I'd been to sea,
Oh, mind what I do say;
The past six months I'd been to sea,
And, boys, this maid looked good to me.
I'll go no more a-roving with you, fair maid.
A-roving, a-roving, etc.

Her cheeks were like the roses red, *etc.*
And her eyes were like twin stars at
    night.
I'll go no more a-roving with you, fair
    maid.
A-roving, a-roving, etc.

I met her walking on the strand, *etc.*
I said 'ahoy' and took her hand.
I'll go no more a-roving with you, fair
    maid.
A-roving, a-roving, etc.

She said, 'Young man, you're rather
    free,' *etc.*
And then turned around and walked
    with me.
I'll go no more a-roving with you, fair
    maid.
A-roving, a-roving, etc.

I took this fair maid for a walk, *etc.*
And we had such a lovin' talk.
I'll go no more a-roving with you, fair
    maid.
A-roving, a-roving, etc.

She swore that she'd be true to me, *etc.*
But she spent my pay so fast and free.
I'll go no more a-roving with you, fair
    maid.
A-roving, a-roving, etc.

Now scarce had I been gone to see, *etc.*
When a soldier took her on his knee.
I'll go no more a-roving with you, fair
    maid.
A-roving, a-roving, etc.

Charlie, etc.
As he cam' marchin' up the street,
The pipes play'd loud and clear;
And a' the folk cam' rinnin' out
To meet the Chevalier.
Oh! Charlie, etc.

Charlie, etc.
Wi' Hieland bonnets on their heads,
And claymores bright and clear,
They cam' to fight for Scotland's right
And the young Chevalier.
Oh! Charlie, etc.

Charlie, etc.
They've left their bonnie Hieland hills,
Their wives and bairnies dear,
To draw the sword for Scotland's Lord,
The young Chevalier.
Oh! Charlie, etc.

Charlie, etc.
Oh! there were mony beating hearts,
And mony a hope and fear;
And mony were the pray'rs put up
For the young Chevalier.
Oh! Charlie, etc.

WILL YE NO COME BACK AGAIN?

LADY NAIRN

1. Bon-nie Char-lie's now a-wa', Safe-ly owre the friend-ly main;

Mo-ny a heart will break in twa, Should he ne'er come back a-gain.

Will ye no come back a-gain? Will ye no come back a-gain?

Bet-ter loved ye can-na be— Will ye no come back a-gain?

Ye trusted in your Hieland men,
They trusted you, dear Charlie;
They kent your hiding in the glen,
Death or exile braving.
Will ye no come back again? etc.

English bribes were a' in vain,
Tho' puir, and puirer, we maun be;
Silla canna buy the heart
That beats aye for thine and thee.
Will ye no come back again? etc.

We watched thee in the gloaming hour,
We watched thee in the morning grey;
Tho' thirty thousand pound they gie,
Oh, there is nane that wad betray!
Will ye no come back again? etc.

Sweet's the laverock's note and lang,
Lilting wildly up the glen;
But aye to me he sings ae sang:
'Will ye no come back again?'
Will ye no come back again? etc.

ROBERT BURNS

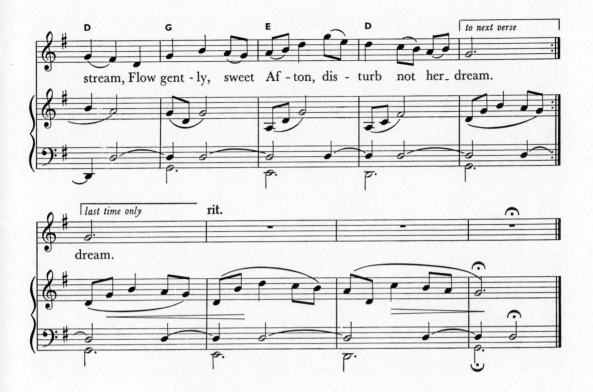

stream, Flow gent - ly, sweet Af - ton, dis - turb not her_ dream.

dream.

Thou stock-dove, whose echo resounds thro' the glen,
Ye wild whistling blackbirds in yon thorny den,
Thou green-crested lapwing, thy screaming forbear,
I charge you disturb not my slumbering fair.

How lofty, sweet Afton, thy neighbouring hills,
Far marked with the courses of clear winding rills;
There daily I wander as morn rises high,
My flocks and my Mary's sweet cot in my eye.

How pleasant thy banks and green valleys below,
Where wild in the woodlands the primroses blow;
There oft as mild ev'ning creeps over the lea,
The sweet-scented birk shades my Mary and me.

Thy crystal stream, Afton, how lovely it glides
And winds by the cot where my Mary resides;
How wanton thy waters her snowy feet lave
As gath'ring sweet flow'rets she stems thy clear wave.

Repeat verse 1

Well sing'st thou cuck - oo, Nor ___ cease thou ne - ver now.

when last voice is finished

★The two lower parts may be sung throughout or alternatively they may be played on the piano or any available instruments.

Sing cuck-oo now, sing cuck-oo. *etc.*

Sing cuck-oo now, sing cuck-oo. *etc.*

Quite fast, with freedom

mf smoothly

1. My love's an ar-bu-tus By the bor-ders of Lene, So slen-der and shape-ly In her gir-dle of green; And I mea-sure the plea-sure Of her eye's sap-phire sheen, By the

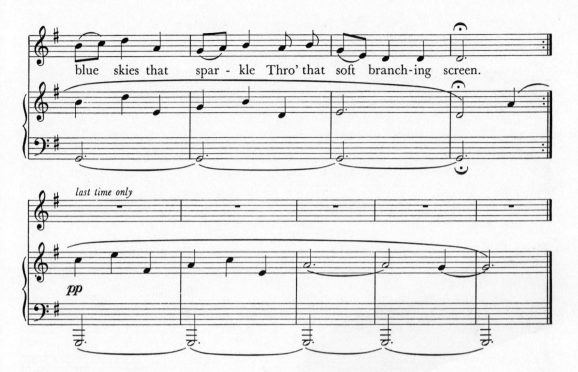

blue   skies that   spar - kle Thro' that soft branch-ing screen.

last time only

pp

But though ruddy the berry
And snowy the flower,
That brighten together
The arbutus bower,
Perfuming and blooming
Through sunshine and shower,
Give me her bright lips
And her laugh's pearly dower.

Alas, fruit and blossom
Shall lie dead on the lea,
And Time's jealous fingers
Dim your young charms, Machree;
But unranging, unchanging,
You'll still cling to me,
Like the evergreen leaf
To the arbutus tree.

Quite fast, cheerfully

with 8ve lower ad lib. in some verses

1. When I was bound ap - pren - tice in fa - mous Lin - coln - shire,_____ Full well I served my mas - ter for more than se - ven year,_____ Till I took up to poach - ing, as

you shall quick-ly hear. Oh! 'tis my de-light on a

shin-ing night, In the sea-son of the year. year.

As me and my companions were setting
  of a snare,
'Twas then we spied the gamekeeper –
  for him we did not care,
For we can wrestle and fight, my
  boys, and jump o'er anywhere.
Oh, 'tis my delight, etc.

As me and my companions were setting
  four or five,
And taking on 'em up again, we
  caught a hare alive,
We took the hare alive, my boys, and
  through the woods did steer.
Oh, 'tis my delight, etc.

I threw him on my shoulder, and
  then we trudged home,
We took him to a neighbour's house
  and sold him for a crown,
We sold him for a crown, my boys,
  but I did not tell you where.
Oh, 'tis my delight, etc.

Success to every gentleman that lives
  in Lincolnshire,
Success to every poacher that wants
  to sell a hare,
Bad luck to every gamekeeper that
  will not sell his deer.
Oh, 'tis my delight, etc.

LANDLORD, FILL THE FLOWING BOWL

Moderate tempo

VERSES 1, 2 & 6

1. Land - lord, fill the flow - ing bowl Un - til it doth run
2. The man who drinks cold wa. - ter pure And goes to bed quite
6. The lit - tle boy who gets a kiss And runs and tells his

to CHORUS

o - ver, Land-lord, fill the flow-ing bowl Un - til it doth run o - ver.
so - ber, Falls_ as the leaves do fall So ear - ly in Oc - to - ber.
bro - ther, Does a ve - ry use-ful thing And bro-ther gets a - no - ther.

VERSES 3 & 5

3. The man who drinks good whisk-ey clear And goes to bed right mel - low,
5. The lit - tle girl who gets a kiss And runs and tells her mo - ther,

to CHORUS

Lives as he ought to live And dies a jol-ly good fel - low.
Does a ve - ry fool-ish thing And sel-dom gets_ a - no - ther.

to CHORUS

★Descant recorders and other melody instruments can play the top line of the piano part, cellos and low instruments can play the bottom line.

32

VERSE 4

4. But he who drinks just what he likes And get-teth half seas o - ver,

Lives un - til he dies, per-haps And then lies down in clo - ver.

CHORUS

For to-night we'll mer - ry be, *For to-night we'll mer - ry be,*

ff

PERCUSSION

a tempo

For to-night we'll mer ry be, *To - mor-row we'll be so - ber.*

33

DIE LORELEI

HEINRICH HEINE

FRIEDRICH SILCHER

1. Ich weiss nicht, was soll es be-deu-ten, dass ich so trau-rig bin,____ Ein Mär-chen aus ur-al-ten Zei-ten, das kommt mir nicht aus dem Sinn.____ Die Luft__ is kühl, und es dun-kelt, und ru-hig fliesst der Rhein,__ Der

Gip - fel des Ber - ges fun - kelt im A - bend-son - nen - schein.

Die schönste Jungfrau sitzt dort oben wunderbar,
Ihr goldnes Geschmeide blitzet, sie kämmt ihr goldenes Haar.
Sie kämmt es mit goldenem Kamme, und singt ein Lied dabei,
Das hat eine wundersame gewaltige Melodei.

Den Schiffer im kleinen Schiffe ergreift es mit wildem Weh,
Er schaut nicht die Felsenriffe, er schaut nur hinauf in die Höh'!
Ich glaube, die Wellen verschlingen am Ende Schiffer und Kahn,
Und das hat mit ihrem Singen, die Lorelei getan.

Heine retells the legend of the Lorelei: a beautiful maiden who from high above the
Rhine lures sailors to their death on the rocks with her singing.

MUSS I DENN

German

Moderate tempo

mf smoothly

1. Muss i denn, muss i denn zum Städ - te -le naus, Städ - te -le naus, und du, mei Schatz, bleibst hier. Wenn i komm, wenn i komm, wenn i wie - der-um komm, Wie - der-um komm, kehr i ein, mein Schatz, bei dir. Kann i

glei — net all-weil bei dir sein, Han i doch mei Freud an dir. Wenn i komm, wenn i komm, wenn i wie-der-um komm, Wie-der-um komm, kehr i ein, mein Schatz, bei dir.

Wie du weinst, wie du weinst, dass i wandere muss,
Wandere muss, wie wenn d'Lieb jetzt wär vorbei.
Sind au drauss, sind au drauss der Mädele viel,
Mädele viel, lieber Schatz, i bleib dir treu.
Denk du net, wenn i andre seh,
Nun sei mei Lieb vorbei.
Sind au drauss, sind au drauss der Mädele viel,
Mädele viel, lieber Schatz, i bleib dir treu.

Übers Jahr, übers jahr, wenn mer Träubele schneid't,
  Träubele schneid't, stell i hier mi wiedrum ein;
Bin i dann, bin i dann dein Schätzele noch,
Schätzele noch, so soll die Hochzeit sein.
Übers Jahr, da ist mein Zeit vorbei,
Da g'hör i mein und dein,
Bin i dann, bin i dann dein Schätzele noch,
Schätzele noch, so soll die Hochzeit sein.

The young man promises to remain true to his girl friend while he is away,
serving his apprenticeship, and to marry her on his return.

With freedom

1. O__ hang-man, O hang-man, O hold up your rope, And hold it__ for a - while, I think I__ see my fa - ther__ dear A - com - ing a ma - ny long mile.

O father, O father, O have you any gold,
Or silver to pay my fee?
They say I've stolen a silver cup
And hanged I must be.

No daughter, no daughter, I've got no gold for thee,
Nor silver to pay your fee;
But I've come here to see you hang
On yon high gallows tree.

The verses may be continued with 'mother', 'brother', 'sister' and finally 'true love'
substituted for 'father'. The last verse runs thus:

Yes, true love, yes, true love, I have got gold for thee,
And silver to pay your fee,
And I've come here to win your neck
From yon high gallows tree.

Manx

Quite slow

1. Lit - tle red bird of the lone - ly moor,

Lone - ly moor, lone - ly moor, Lit - tle red bird of the

lone - ly moor, O where did you sleep __ last night? ____

Out on a gorse - bush dark and wide, Dark and wide,

dark and wide, Swift rain___ was fall - ing on ev - 'ry side. O hard was my sleep___ last night.___

Little red bird of the lonely moor, etc.
Did I not sleep on a swaying briar,
Swaying briar, swaying briar,
Tossing about as the wind rose higher?
O hard was my sleep last night.

Little red bird of the lonely moor, etc.
Did I not sleep on a cold wave's crest,
Cold wave's crest, cold wave's crest,
Where many a man has taken his rest?
O hard was my sleep last night.

Little red bird of the lonely moor, etc.
Wrapp'd in two leaves I lay at ease,
Lay at ease, lay at ease,
As sleeps the young babe on its mother's knees.
O sweet was my sleep last night.

THE FIDDLERS

Ukrainian

★If there are violins and recorders playing, the pianist need play only the left-hand part.

42

On the hills the cows are grazing,
I must go, it's time for milking,
Oh, oh, oh!
I must go, it's time for milking,
Oh, oh, oh!

I will take the milk and butter,
Give it to the fiddlers playing,
Ho, oh, oh!
Give it to the fiddlers playing,
Oh, oh, oh!

CINDY

1. You ought to see my Cin - dy, She lives way down south; She's so sweet the hon - ey bees Swarm a - round her mouth.

CHORUS

Get a - long home, *Get a - long* home, *Get a - long home, Cin - dy,*

Cin - dy, I'll mar-ry you_ some day.

The first I seen my Cindy,
She was standing in the door,
Her shoes and stockings in her hand,
With her feet all over the floor.
Get along home, etc.

She took me to the parlour,
She cooled me with her fan,
She swore I was the prettiest thing
In the shape of mortal man.
Get along home, etc.

She told me that she loved me,
She called me sugar plum;
She throwed her arms around me,
I thought my time had come.
Get along home, etc.

I wish I was an apple
A-hangin' on a tree,
And every time my Cindy passed
She'd take a bite of me.
Get along home, etc.

And if I was a sugar tree
A-standin' in the town,
Every time my Cindy passed
I'd shake some sugar down.
Get along home, etc.

And if I was a needle,
As fine as I could sew,
I'd sew myself to her coat tails
And down the road I'd go.
Get along home, etc.

Oh, Cindy is a pretty girl,
Cindy is a peach.
She throwed her arms around my neck
And hung on like a leach.
Get along home, etc.

Cindy got religion,
I'll tell you what she done,
She walked up to the preacher
And chawed her chewing gum.
Get along home, etc.

So full of her religion,
She went preachin' round the town,
She got so full of glory,
She shook her stockings down.
Get along home, etc.

Cindy in the springtime,
Cindy in the fall,
If I can't have my Cindy,
I'll have no gal at all.
Get along home, etc.

American

Moderate tempo, with variety

1. The most chi – val – rous fish of the o – cean,_____ To

la – dies for – bear-ing and mild,_____ Though his re-cord be dark, is the

man – eat – ing shark Who will eat nei – ther wo – man nor child._____

He dines upon seamen and skippers,
And tourists his hunger assuage.
And a fresh cabin boy will inspire him with joy
If he's past the maturity age.

A doctor, a lawyer, a preacher,
He'll gobble one any fine day,
But the ladies, God bless 'em, he'll only address 'em
Politely and go on his way.

I can readily cite you an instance
Where a lovely young lady of Breem,
Who was tender and sweet and delicious to eat,
Fell into the bay with a scream.

She struggled and flounced in the water
And signalled in vain for her bark,
And she'd surely been drowned if she hadn't been found
By a chivalrous man-eating shark.

He bowed in a manner most polished,
Thus soothing her impulses wild;
'Don't be frightened,' he said, 'I've been properly bred
And will eat neither woman nor child.'

Then he proffered his fin and she took it—
Such a gallantry none can dispute—
While the passengers cheered as the vessel they neared
And a broadside was fired in salute.

And they stood alongside the vessel,
When a life-saving dinghy was lowered
With the pick of the crew, and her relatives too,
And the mate and the skipper aboard.

So they took her aboard in a jiffy,
And the shark stood at attention the while,
Then he raised on his flipper and ate up the skipper
And went on his way with a smile.

And this shows that the prince of the ocean,
To ladies forbearing and mild,
Though his record be dark, is the man-eating shark
Who will eat neither woman nor child.

SIMPLE GIFTS

Fairly slow

American

'Tis the gift to be sim-ple, 'tis the gift to be free, 'Tis the gift to come down where you ought to be; And when we find our-selves in the place just right, 'Twill be

in the val-ley of love and de-light. *When true sim-pli-ci-ty is gained, To*

bow and to bend we shan't be a-shamed. To turn, turn will

be our de-light, Till by turn-ing, turn-ing we come out right.

EVERY NIGHT WHEN THE SUN GOES IN

American

1.Ev -'ry night _____ when the sun goes in, _____

CHORUS: *True love, don't weep; _____ True love, don't mourn,*

— *True love, don't weep; _____ True love, don't mourn,*

Ev -'ry night _____ when the sun goes in, _____

— *True love, don't weep; _____ True love, don't mourn,*

Ev -'ry night _____ when the sun goes in, _____

I wish to the Lord that train would come,
I wish to the Lord that train would come,
I wish to the Lord that train would come,
To take me back to where I come from.
True love, etc.

It's once my apron hung down low,
It's once my apron hung down low,
It's once my apron hung down low,
He'd follow me through sleet and snow.
True love, etc.

It's now my apron's to my chin,
It's now my apron's to my chin,
It's now my apron's to my chin,
He'll face my door and won't come in.
True love, etc.

I wish to the Lord my babe was born,
A' sitting upon his papa's knee,
And me, poor girl, was dead and gone,
And the green grass growing over me.
True love, etc.

American

Put in your water and shovel in your coal,
Put your head out the window,
Watch the drivers roll.
'I'll run her till she leaves the rail
'Cause we're eight hours late with the Western Mail.'
He looked at his watch and his watch was slow,
Looked at the water and the water was low,
Turned to his fireboy, then he said,
'We're bound to reach 'Frisco
But we'll all be dead.'
Casey Jones, etc.

Casey pulled up Reno Hill,
Tooted at the crossing
With an awful shrill.
'Snakes' all knew by the engine's moans
That the hogger at the throttle was Casey Jones.
He pulled up short two miles from the place,
Freight train stared him right in the face,
Turned to his fireboy, 'Son, you'd better jump
'Cause there's two locomotives
That are going to bump.'
Casey Jones, etc.

Casey said just before he died
'There's two more roads
I'd like to ride.'
Fireboy asked, 'What can they be?'
'The Rio Grande and the Sante Fe.'
Mrs. Jones sat on her bed a sigh'n,
Had a pink that her Casey was dy'n,
Said, 'Hush you children, stop your cry'n,
'Cause you'll get another Papa
On the Salt Lake Line.'
Casey Jones, etc.

I have stockings of silk,
Shoes of fine green leather,
Combs to buckle my hair,
And a ring for every finger.

Feather beds are soft,
And painted rooms are bonny,
But I would trade them all
For my handsome, winsome Johnny.

I know where I'm goin'
And I know who's goin' with me;
I know who I love,
But the dear knows who I'll marry!

Some say he's black,
But I say he's bonny;
Fairest of them all
Is my handsome, winsome Johnny.

HUSH-YOU-BYE

American

Gently, fairly slow

SMALL BELLS or GLOCKENSPIEL

1. Hush - you - bye, Don't you cry, Go to sleep my lit-tle ba - by. When you wake, You shall have cake, An' drive those pret-ty lit-tle

56

hor - ses. Blacks an' bays, Dap-ples an' grays,

Coach an' six-a lit-tle hor - ses.

Rock-a-bye,
Don't you cry,
Go to sleep my little baby.
Send you to school
Ridin' on a mule
An' drivin' those pretty little horses.
Blacks an' bays,
Dapples an' grays,
Coach an' six-a little horses.

Yugoslavian

1. Come, you lit - tle ras - cal, Rock the ba - by's cra - dle,

Make your - self more use - ful, Sure - ly you are a - ble.

No! he said, I shall not,___ Shall not rock the ba - by.

Come, you little idler,
Off to school I'll take you.
No! he said, you'll never —
Quickly I'll escape you.
Lessons are so dreary,
Only girls delight me.

LULLABY, MY JAMIE

Latvian

Smoothly

1. Lul - la - by, my Ja - mie,

Soft - ly sleep-ing child, Gent - ly mo - ther rocks you,

Light her hands and mild.

Snow-white lambs for Jamie,
Soon they will be shorn,
And their softest wool shall
Always keep you warm.

Horses drew the carriage
On your christening day,
God grant six fine steeds
To speed you on your way.

FRÈRE JACQUES

French

Frè - re   Jac - ques,   frè - re   Jac - ques,   dor - mez -

vous,   dor - mez - vous?   Son - nez les ma - ti - nes,   son - nez les ma -

- ti - nes,   Din,   din,   don!   din,   din,   don!

CHEVALIERS DE LA TABLE RONDE

Not too fast, but with energy

French

Che - va - li - ers de la ta - ble ronde, Gou - tons voir si le vin est bon.

faster

Gou-tons voir, oui, oui, oui, Gou-tons voir, non, non, non,

first tempo

Gou - tons voir si le vin est bon.

faster

Gou - tons voir, oui, oui, oui, Gou - tons

voir, non, non, non, Gou-tons voir si le vin est bon.

S'il est bon, s'il est agréable,
J'en boirai jusqu'à mon plaisir.   } (twice)
J'en boirai, oui, oui, oui,
J'en boirai, non, non, non,
J'en boirai jusqu'à mon plaisir.   } ,,

J'en boirai cinq ou six bouteilles,   } ,,   Et les quatre plus grands ivrognes   } (twice)
Une femme sur les genoux.   Porteront les quat' coins du drap.
Une femme, oui, oui, oui,   Porteront, oui, oui, oui,
Une femme, non, non, non,   } ,,   Porteront, non, non, non,   } ,,
Une femme sur les genoux.   Porteront les quat' coins du drap.

Toc, toc, toc, on frappe à la porte, } ,,   Les deux pieds contre la muraille   } ,,
Je crois bien que c'est son mari.   Et la tête sous le robinet.
Je crois bien, oui, oui, oui,   Et la tête, oui, oui, oui,
Je crois bien, non, non, non,   } ,,   Et la tête, non, non, non,   } ,,
Je crois bien que c'est son mari.   Et la tête sous le robinet.

Si c'est lui, que le diable l'emporte, } ,,   Sur ma tombe je veux qu'on inscrive } ,,
Car il vient troubler mon plaisir.   'Ici git le roi des bouvers.'
Car il vient, oui, oui, oui,   Ici git, oui, oui, oui,
Car il vient, non, non, non,   } ,,   Ici git, non, non, non,   } ,,
Car il vient troubler mon plaisir.   Ici git le roi des bouvers.

Si je meurs, je veux qu'on m'enterre } ,,   La morale de cette histoire,   } ,,
Dans la cave où il y a du bon vin.   C'est à boire avant de mourir.
Dans la cave, oui, oui, oui,   C'est à boire, oui, oui, oui,
Dans la cave, non, non, non,   } ,,   C'est à boire, non, non, non,   } ,,
Dans la cave où il y a du bon vin.   C'est à boire avant de mourir.

EN PASSANT PAR LA LORRAINE

French

With movement

1. En pas-sant par la Lor-raine,_ A - vec mes sa - bots!_

J'ai trou-vé trois Cap-it-aines_ A - vec mes sa -

- bots, Ton-taine!_ Oh! oh! oh!_ A - vec mes sa - bots.

J'ai trouvé trois Capitaines, } *(twice)*
Avec mes sabots!
Ils m'ont appelé' vilaine,
Avec mes sabots, etc.

Ils m'ont appelé' vilaine, } „
Avec mes sabots!
Je ne suis pas si vilaine,
Avec mes sabots, etc.

Je ne suis pas si vilaine, } „
Avec mes sabots!
Puisque le fils du Roi m'aime,
Avec mes sabots, etc.

Puisque le fils du Roi m'aime, } *(twice)*
Avec mes sabots!
Il m'a donné pour étrenne,
Avec mes sabots, etc.

Un bouquet de marjolaine, } *(twice)*
Avec mes sabots!
S'il fleurit je serai Reine,
Avec mes sabots, etc.

Il m'a donné pour étrenne, } „
Avec mes sabots!
Un bouquet de marjolaine,
Avec mes sabots, etc.

S'il fleurit je serai Reine, } „
Avec mes sabots!
Mais s'il meurt je perds ma peine,
Avec mes sabots, etc.

In reply to the mocking of three captains, the singer replies that she is loved by the King's son who gave her a bunch of marjoram for New Year. If it flowers she will be Queen; if it doesn't she won't!

BLOW THE MAN DOWN

Not too fast

1. Blow the man down, bul - lies, blow the man down, And a -
way, _____ hey, *blow the man down.*
Blow the man down on the top of his crown.
Give me some time to blow the man down.

'Twas on board a Black Baller I first served my time,
And away, hey, blow the man down.
And on the Black Baller I wasted my prime.
Give me some time to blow the man down.

It's when a Black Baller is clear of the land,
And away, hey, blow the man down.
Our bosun then gives us the word of command.
Give me some time to blow the man down.

'Lay aft!' is the cry 'to the break of the poop!'
And away, hey, blow the man down.
'Or I'll help you along with the toe of my boot.'
Give me some time to blow the man down.

Pay attention to orders, yes, you, one and all,
And away, hey, blow the man down.
For see right above you there flies the Black Ball.
Give me some time to blow the man down.

It's when a Black Baller comes down to the dock,
And away, hey, blow the man down.
The lasses and lads to the pier-heads do flock.
Give me some time to blow the man down.

Put him in the long boat till he's sober, etc.
Way, Hey, etc.

Pull out the plug and wet him all over, etc.
Way, Hey, etc.

Put him in the bilge and make him drink it, etc.
Way, Hey, etc.

Put him in a leaky boat and make him bale her, etc.
Way, Hey, etc.

Tie him to the scuppers with the hose pipe on him, etc.
Way, Hey, etc.

Tie him to the topmast when she's yardarm under, etc.
Way, Hey, etc.

Heave him by the leg in a runnin' bowlin'! etc.
Way, Hey, etc.

Temperance lectures will never help him, etc.
Way, Hey, etc.

Give him a hair of the dog that bit him, etc.
Way, Hey, etc.

Usually ending with:
That's what we'll do with the drunken sailor,
That's what we'll do with the drunken sailor,
That's what we'll do with the drunken sailor,
Early in the morning.
Way, Hey, etc.

RIO GRANDE

American

With movement

1.Oh, were___ you e - ver in Ri - o Grande? *A - way Ri - o!___* Oh, were__ you e - ver on___ that strand? *For we're bound for the Ri o Grande,* And a-

way Ri - o! 'Way Ri-o! So fare you well, my

bon - ny young girl For we're bound for the Ri - o Grande.

You Liverpool ladies, we'd have you to know,
Away Rio!
We're bound to the South'ard, come on, let us go.
For we're bound, etc.

Sing good-bye to Sally and good-bye to Sue,
And all who are listening, good-bye to you!

Man the capstan and run it around,
We'll heave up the anchor to that jolly sound.

Heave with will, and heave long, and heave strong,
And sing a good chorus, for 'tis a good song.

Oh the anchor is weighed and the sails they are set,
The maids that we're leaving, we'll never forget.

We've a jolly good ship and a jolly good crew,
A jolly good mate and a good skipper, too.

SHENANDOAH

American

Rather slow

1. Oh, Shen-an-doah,— I long to see you,— A - way, you roll-ing ri - ver,— Oh, Shen-an-doah,— I long to see you. A - way, we're bound a - way, 'Cross the wide Mis-sou - ri.

Oh, Shenandoah's my native valley.
Away, you rolling river,
Oh, Shenandoah's my native valley.
Away, we're bound away,
'Cross the wide Missouri.

Oh, Shenandoah, it's far I wander.
Away, you rolling river,
Oh, Shenandoah, it's far I wander.
Away, we're bound away,
'Cross the wide Missouri.

Oh, Shenandoah has rushing waters.
Away, you rolling river,
Oh, Shenandoah has rushing waters.
Away, we're bound away,
'Cross the wide Missouri.

Oh, Shenandoah, I long to hear you.
Away, you rolling river,
Oh, Shenandoah, I long to hear you.
Away, we're bound away,
'Cross the wide Missouri.

Oh, Shenandoah, I love your daughter.
Away, you rolling river,
Oh, Shenandoah, I love your daughter.
Away, we're bound away,
'Cross the wide Missouri.

Oh, Shenandoah, I'll never leave you.
Away, you rolling river,
Oh, Shenandoah, I'll never leave you.
Away, we're bound away,
'Cross the wide Missouri.

Oh, Shenandoah, I'll never grieve you.
Away, you rolling river,
Oh, Shenandoah, I'll never grieve you.
Away, we're bound away,
'Cross the wide Missouri.

TO PORTSMOUTH

DAVID MELVILL
Book of Roundels 1612

Moderately fast

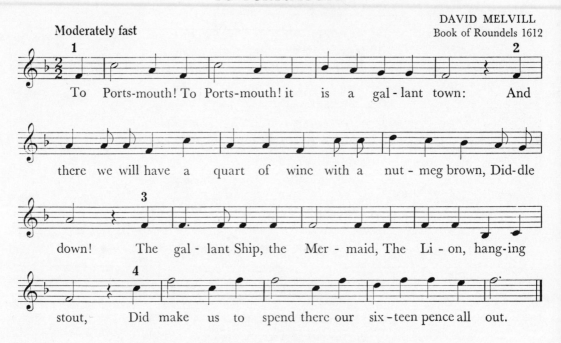

To Ports-mouth! To Ports-mouth! it is a gal-lant town: And

there we will have a quart of wine with a nut-meg brown, Did-dle

down! The gal-lant Ship, the Mer-maid, The Li-on, hang-ing

stout, Did make us to spend there our six-teen pence all out.

KOOKABURRA

Australian

Koo-ka-bur-ra sits on an old gum tree,— Mer-ry, mer-ry king of the bush is he;— Laugh, koo-ka-bur-ra, laugh, koo-ka-bur-ra, Gay your life must be.

★If you are singing this as a round the 2nd voice enters two bars after the 1st voice, i.e. when the 1st voice has reached the asterisk.

THE STREETS OF FORBES

Australian

Come all you Lach-lan men, and a sor-row-ful tale I'll tell Con- cer-ning of a he - ro bold who thro' mis - for -tune fell. His name it was Ben Hall, a man of good re -nown Who was

hun - ted from his sta - ti - on, and_ like a dog shot_

down.

Three years he roamed the roads, and he showed the traps some fun;
A thousand pound was on his head, with Gilbert and John Dunn.
Ben parted from his comrades, the outlaws did agree
To give away bushranging and to cross the briny sea.

Ben went to Goobang Creek, and that was his downfall;
For riddled like a sieve was valiant Ben Hall.
'Twas early in the morning upon the fifth of May
When the seven police surrounded him as fast asleep he lay.

Bill Dargin he was chosen to shoot the outlaw dead;
The troopers then fired madly, and filled him full of lead.
They rolled him in a blanket, and strapped him to his prad,
And led him through the streets of Forbes to show the prize they had.

BOTANY BAY

There's the Captain as is our Commander,
There's the bo'sun and all the ship's crew,
There's the first and second-class passengers,
Knows what we poor convicts go through.
Singing too-ral, etc.

'Taint leavin' old England we cares about,
'Taint cos we mispels what we knows,
But becos all we light-fingered gentry
Hops around with a log on our toes.
Singing too-ral, etc.

For seven long years I'll be staying here,
For seven long years and a day,
For meeting a cove in an area
And taking his ticker away.
Singing too-ral, etc.

Oh, had I the wings of a turtle-dove!
I'd soar on my pinions so high,
Slap bang to the arms of my Polly love,
And in her sweet presence I'd die.
Singing too-ral, etc.

Now, all my young Dookies and Duchesses,
Take warning from what I've to say,
Mind all is your own as you touchesses,
Or you'll find us in Botany Bay.
Singing too-ral, etc.

1. Oh, I dreamt I shore in a shear-in'-shed, and it was a dream of joy, For ev-'ry one of the rouse-a-bouts was a girl dressed up as a boy. Dressed

up like a page in a pan - to - mime, the pret - ti - est
e - ver seen;_____ They had flax - en hair, they had
coal - black hair and__ ev - 'ry shade be - tween._____

The shed was cooled by electric fans that was over every shoot;
The pens was of polished ma-ho-gany, and everything else to suit;
The huts had springs to the mattresses, and the tucker was simply grand,
And every night by the billabong we danced to a German band.

Our pay was the wool on the jumbuck's backs, so we shore till all was blue—
The sheep was washed afore they was shore (and the rams was scented too);
And we all of us wept when the shed cut out, in spite of the long, hot days,
For every hour them girls waltzed in with whisky and beer on trays!

There was three of them girls to every chap, and as jealous as they could be—
There was three of them girls to every chap, and six of 'em picked on me;
We was draftin' 'em out for the homeward track and sharin' 'em round like steam,
When I woke with my head in the blazin' sun to find 'twas a shearer's dream.

HEY HO, TO THE GREENWOOD

DAVID MELVILL
Book of Roundels 1612

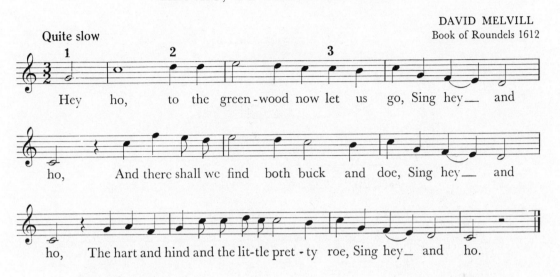

Quite slow

Hey ho, to the green-wood now let us go, Sing hey___ and

ho, And there shall we find both buck and doe, Sing hey___ and

ho, The hart and hind and the lit-tle pret-ty roe, Sing hey___ and ho.

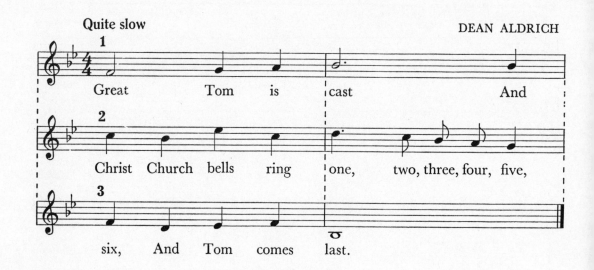

Quite slow

DEAN ALDRICH

Great Tom is cast And

Christ Church bells ring one, two, three, four, five,

six, And Tom comes last.

TURN AGAIN WHITTINGTON

Moderate tempo

Turn a - gain Whit - ting - ton

thou worth - y ci - ti - zen

Lord Mayor of Lon - don.

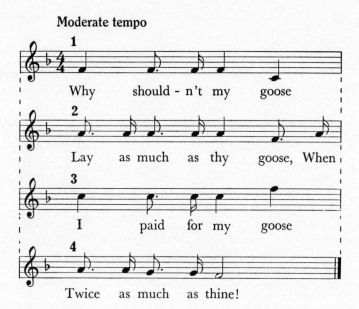

MY DAME HATH A LAME TAME CRANE

MATTHEW WHITE

My dame hath a lame tame crane, My dame hath a crane that is lame; Pray, gen-tle Jane, let my dame's lame tame crane Feed and come home a-gain.

Moderate tempo

1. Sweet - ly sings the don - key at the break of day.

2. If you don't sing loud - er, you will get no hay.____ Hee-

3. - haw! Hee-haw! Hee-haw, hee-haw, hee-haw!

EPIGRAM ON SINGERS

SAMUEL TAYLOR COLERIDGE

Rather slow

Swans _____ sing ___ be - fore __ they __ die ____ 'twere

no bad thing Should cer -tain per-sons die

be - fore they sing. _____

COME HERE AND SING!

W. A. MOZART

Come here and sing! Come now! Sing now!

Come here and sing now! But sing both clear and

bright-ly, Creak and croak not like a —! Tra-la-la-la-la-la-

la-ri-da, Tra-la-la-la-la-la-la-ri-da,

Yes, that now sounds ve-ry good, Tra-la-la-la-la-la-

la-ri-da, Tra-la-la-la-la-la-la-ri-da.

DONA NOBIS PACEM

1 Do - na no - bis pa - cem, pa - cem, Do - na -

2 no - bis pa - cem, Do - na no - bis pa - cem,

3 Do - na no - bis pa - cem, Do - na no - bis

pa - cem, Do - na no - bis pa - cem.

THOMAS TALLIS

Slow and dignified

1. Glo - ry to Thee, my God, this night For all the bles - sings of the light; Keep me, O keep me, King of kings, Be - neath Thy own al - migh - ty wings.

Forgive me, Lord, for Thy dear Son,
The ill that I this day have done,
That with the world, myself, and Thee,
I, ere I sleep, at peace may be.

Teach me to live, that I may dread
The grave as little as my bed;
Teach me to die, that so I may
Rise glorious at the awful day.

O may my soul on Thee repose,
And with sweet sleep mine eyelids close,
Sleep that may me more vigorous make
To serve my God when I awake.

When in the night I sleepless lie,
My soul with heavenly thoughts supply;
Let no ill dreams disturb my rest,
No powers of darkness me molest.

You, my blest guardian, whilst I sleep
Close to my bed your vigils keep;
Divine love into me instil,
Stop all the avenues of ill.

Praise God, from whom all blessings flow,
Praise him, all creatures here below,
Praise him above, ye heavenly host,
Praise Father, Son, and Holy Ghost.

INDEX OF TITLES

INDEX OF FIRST LINES